Presented to:

By: Heather

Nino

Friendship is a long, sweet prayer made
up of kind acts that reach heavenward.
HEATHER HARPHAM KOPP

Women are
Sisters at Heart

Celebrating the Joys of Friendship

MELODY CARLSON

This book is lovingly dedicated to my special Sisters at Heart:

Melisa, Robin, Renee, Carol, Nancy, Elizabeth, Londy, Janet, Joyce, Julia, Karla, Peggy, Joyce, Luanne, Carla, Pam, Cheryl, Audrey, Yuan, Isobel, Kathy, Heather, Linda, Sara, Lonnie, Jennifer, Sue, Anne, Connie, Patsy, Kate, Carol, Lydia, Deb, Milo, Erikka, Heidi, Bridget, Raelyn, Eva …and the list goes on and on and on.

soul sisters

friendship is . . . one soul in two bodies.
PYTHAGORAS

a woman like me!

You feel the connection almost instantly—it's as if your souls are similar somehow.

You've only just met and barely exchanged a few sentences, yet it's as if you're in sync—on the same wavelength. Your eyes meet with a spark of recognition and somehow *you both know:* this is a woman I can relate to. This woman understands who I am. This is a woman like me!

Anne Shirley (*Anne of Green Gables*) described her dear friend Diana as a "bosom friend and a kindred spirit." Whether you call this person a "best friend," "close confidante," or "soul sister," you know deep within that a special bond exists between you. You know this friendship is sent straight from the hand of God.

A friend like this is a precious treasure—a rare find. Yet, surprisingly, these relationships are not usually fragile. In fact, they may be of the sturdiest sort. Built upon a solid foundation of love, trust, and grace, they can easily stand the test of time and stress.

But we must not take them for granted. For just as a good marriage needs careful tending and maintenance, so does a valuable friendship.

10

As time passes, our interests and focuses are constantly changing, and the need to stay informed and in touch with these special friends increases over the years. But the reward of nurturing such a relationship is well worth the effort.

Because the truth is, there are only a handful of women in this world who are *so much like you*—those kindred spirits who are moved by the same music, love the same books, enjoy the same activities. Like a priceless jewel, they are to be valued, cherished, and—and best of all—*enjoyed!*

When friendships are real, they are not glass threads or frostwork, but the solidest thing we know.
RALPH WALDO EMERSON

A Garden of Friends

Friends are like flowers
That brighten your day
With fragrance and beauty
To share on life's way.

So treat them like flowers
From the Gardener above,
Weed them with mercy
And water with love.

celebrating life

How much tastier is a cup of delicious, gourmet coffee or tea when shared with someone special—someone who savors the taste as much as you do. How much more pleasurable is an incredible art exhibit when a friend comes along who loves Van Gogh as much as you do! Why is it that these experiences are enhanced and magnified when just the right person is there to delight in them with us?

Perhaps because life suddenly becomes a celebration—an occasion to warm the heart. If you think about it, how often do we celebrate in isolation? When something is worth commemorating, we want others to share it with us! And that's just one of the great pleasures that comes with a special friend. She helps us celebrate life more fully—she enriches our experience, adding sparkles and laughter and love!

Jesus surrounded himself with close friends here on earth. And while his purpose was to reveal himself and his ultimate plan for salvation, one can't help but notice that he also enjoyed a good time with his friends. In fact, he often described himself as the bridegroom, saying how it was time to celebrate—to eat, drink, and enjoy his presence.

Good friends are like that. They bring an air of festivity and celebration into an otherwise ordinary day. Life without dear friends is like watching "The Sound of Music" in black and white with the volume turned off—flat and gray and silent.

So, celebrate the divine gift of friendship. Enjoy the color and dimension it brings into your day—and give it back in full return! Life is for living, and friends are one of the most enjoyable ingredients.

Friendship is . . . a present you give yourself.
ROBERT LOUIS STEVENSON

The better part of one's life
consists of . . . friendships.
ABRAHAM LINCOLN

simple pleasures

*D*o you remember how easily you could be entertained as a child, simply with a friend by your side? Just sitting on the front porch discussing who was the cutest boy in the sixth grade could occupy you for hours, as could walking barefoot together on a hot summer's afternoon while quietly slurping a vanilla cone. Somehow, doing nothing with your best friend was an event.

And remember years later when you dropped in on your best friend and shared a cup of stale morning coffee, laughing together as you helped her fold a week's worth of laundry? Somehow, by the time you left, the world seemed a happier place.

That's the beauty of a great friendship — it makes even the mundane parts of life colorful.

Yet how easy it is to neglect a friend. To become so busy and distracted with the daily demands of life that we convince ourselves

there's simply no time left for the enjoyment and rewards of friendship. But how much we miss in life when we fall victim to this line of rationale.

For here's the sad truth: when we decide we don't have time for friends, we're choosing not to live our lives as fully as God intends. We are robbing ourselves and others of one of life's simplest but greatest treasures: friendship.

How many minutes does it take to call a friend on the phone or to meet her for a cup of coffee or a short walk? When we take the time for friendship, we discover that pleasant delights are often found in the simplest packages!

*The best and most beautiful things
in the world cannot be seen or even touched.
They must be felt with the heart.*
HELEN KELLER

TOO BUSY to NOTICE

She hurried past her neighbor,
but had each hair in place.
She rushed through morning traffic
'til she found a parking space.
She only paused a moment
when an old friend called for lunch,
but said she was too busy
and that she had a hunch
she'd have to push through—nonstop—
just to get her work complete.
And who could pause to visit?
And who takes time to eat?
She listened with impatience
when her mother called to say:
"Can you come for dinner?
—Well, perhaps another day?"
What is wrong with people?
Do they think her ife is fun?
It seems that no one understands
all she must get done!
She'll be sitting all alone someday,
(She's the only one to blame)
because she never noticed
hints of friendship when they came.

Building Trust, piece by piece

*N*othing makes us feel quite so vulnerable as placing our heart and soul in the hands of another. Yet this is the level of trust and honesty we long for with our dearest friends—and hope they find with us. For to have a friend is to be a friend; it's impossible to separate one from the other.

And how is this kind of trust achieved? How do we know if our friends are truly trustworthy? How do we know if *we* are?

19

Trust is knowing that you can be transparently honest with your friend. It's the assurance that your deepest secrets, your strongest desires, your biggest dreams, even your worst mistakes are safe in the hands of another. It's believing that your friend will not betray your confidence. It's knowing she has your best interests at heart.

But a foundation of trust is built
slowly, one piece at a time. For only
as we become convinced that one
portion of our life is safe with a
friend, can we hand over
another.

In other words, we don't usually
dump everything about ourselves onto a brand new
friend. We take it slowly and carefully—wisely
revealing only what seems appropriate —until
our confidence in our friend increases along
with her confidence in us.

After awhile, we know without a doubt
that the foundation of trust is strong and firm. We
don't even question it anymore. Instead, we find that
a truly good friend can even discern when we're *not* being
totally honest—with her or with ourselves.

*One of the most beautiful qualities of true friendship
is to understand and to be understood.*
SENECA

*A soul friend is someone with whom
we can share our greatest joys
and deepest fears,
confess our worst sins
and most persistent faults,
clarify our highest hopes
and perhaps most inarticulated dreams.*
EDWARD C. SELLNER

*It is hard to believe
that anything is worthwhile,
unless what is infinitely precious to us
is precious alike to another mind.*
GEORGE ELIOT

earthly sisters

*A sister is . . . a friend and a smile
and a rainbow all rolled into one.*

LAINE PARSONS

a sister of my very own

Perhaps a girl's first "best friend" in life is her very own sister. And yet sisters seldom emerge from childhood and adolescence without a few silly squabbles—not to mention a number of full-blown fights. But the kindness of time erases a myriad of little hurts, and forgiveness seems to flow more abundantly for a sister. After all, she is flesh of my flesh, bone of my bone—in fact, she's an awful lot like me! And we both managed to survive being raised by the same parents in the same house in the same neighborhood!

24

Besides, who else can understand how it felt to be *me* as a child? Who else can relate to me so easily, so completely, so empathetically? Who else, but a sister knows how

"mom drives me crazy sometimes" or cries with me when she hears our favorite old apple tree has been cut down?

Because we grew up together, my sister and I share not only the same gene pool, we share many of the same experiences. We both sobbed when a car hit the cat. We went through chicken pox and measles and sunburns together. We sneaked down late on Christmas Eve to spy on Santa Claus. We built fantastic sandcastles and discovered beautiful seashells on the beach. We marched off to summer camp together—each trying to appear braver than the other.

We tried so hard to be different and separate from each other—searching for our own unique style and personality—yet when all is said and done, we are amazingly alike … as only sisters can be.

Now as grownup sisters, we rejoice over our shared childhood —without her those early memories would feel empty and lonely. How I thank God for my sister and the way we grew up together.

God displays His splendor

In mountains, plains, and seas,

In rich green turf, and pounding surf,

In flowers, birds, and trees;

God displays His beauty

In clear blue skies above,

In daffodils, and sunlit hills,

And in my sister's love.

shared moments and memories

So many shared memories rest between sisters. Some, like a sleeping grizzly bear, seem best left undisturbed. While others can fill a rainy afternoon with laughter and sunshine. For sisters have shared it all—the good, the bad, and everything inbetween. We both remember the time the dog got carsick on the way to the beach and the time Uncle Harry forgot to put his new Pontiac into park. We remember the night mother cried, and the following morning when we served her

27

breakfast in bed: burnt toast and soggy Cheerios. Or the time Grandma made a big pot of clam chowder from the razor clams we'd dug ourselves.

These poignant memories are the stuff childhood is made of—and who better to share them with than a sister!

Even the difficult memories grow
softer, gentler, when shared with a
sister who understands as you
do. The tragedies, the losses,
the heartbreaks aren't quite so
harsh and cruel when you
remember how you both cried and

suffered together—how you comforted each other.

But sisters don't always remember everything
in the same way. And that, in itself, can be a blessing.
For a sister can enlarge our limited perspective
when she shares from her own. An incident we
perceived as a failure or embarrassment can
suddenly take on a whole new light when seen
through a sister's eyes.

Without a doubt, childhood memories contain more
vivid colors, greater textures, and more meaning when shared
with a sister ... when remembered together.

You know full as well as I do the value of sisters' affection to each other; there is nothing like it in this earth.

CHARLOTTE BRONTE

always There for me

*I*t seems as if children live in a world all their own, separate from their parents, older relatives, and other grownups. And in my childhood world—in my childish eyes—problems appeared large, challenges urgent, and needs pressing. Yet the adults barely take notice.

Those were the times when my sister was there for me. She was willing to crawl beneath the house when it seemed the most important thing on earth to find a lost guinea pig.

31

She understood when I *had* to find just the perfect red belt to go with my red shoes. And only she knew the vital importance of demonstrating for me, step-by-step, how to embroider a daisy on my blue jeans. She understood the significance of these things. She was there for me.

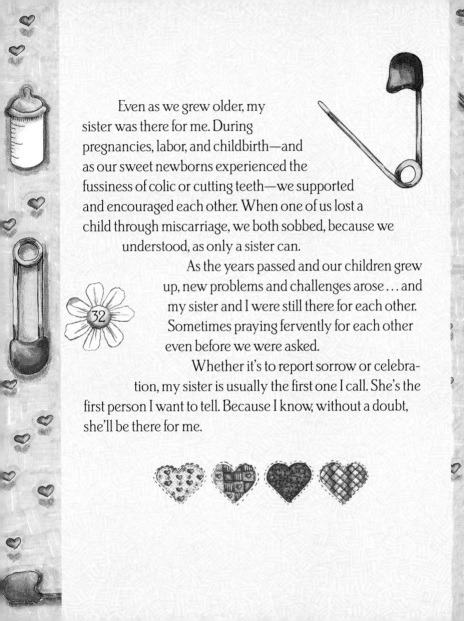

Even as we grew older, my sister was there for me. During pregnancies, labor, and childbirth—and as our sweet newborns experienced the fussiness of colic or cutting teeth—we supported and encouraged each other. When one of us lost a child through miscarriage, we both sobbed, because we understood, as only a sister can.

As the years passed and our children grew up, new problems and challenges arose … and my sister and I were still there for each other. Sometimes praying fervently for each other even before we were asked.

Whether it's to report sorrow or celebration, my sister is usually the first one I call. She's the first person I want to tell. Because I know, without a doubt, she'll be there for me.

32

It is a wonderful feeling to know
I have a sister I can depend on,
one who has stood beside me
through everything,
who loves me just for who I am,
and who means more to me
than I can ever express.
There aren't many people
who have gone through all
that we have together
and emerged with a bond
as strong as ours.

SUSAN HICKMAN SATER

our lives connect

*I*s there some silent vow of sisterhood—some secret page taken from the book of childhood—a promise we both made without even knowing it? For the way that sisters' hearts unite is a true mystery. Even sisters themselves cannot fully explain, or even understand, it. But it's there. And it's real. We are loyal—fiercely so. And yet, we don't hesitate to point out each other's flaws or blind spots—sometimes bluntly. But oh, how we are able to forgive—totally and completely. Perhaps it's because we are so alike, so connected. It's as if we're simply forgiving ourselves.

Let's promise each other, dear sister, that we'll always be ready to listen, able to love, and quick to forgive. Let's reaffirm our commitment to sisterhood, and make sure we never allow any offense, whether big or small, to come between us or divide us. For there's no one on earth quite like a sister. And even one day lost to resentment or bitterness is one day too many.

God planned for our lives to connect. Let's make sure we keep it that way.

*A sister is . . . like a breath
of spring through the storms
of winter . . . a guiding star
in the darkness of night.*

GERI DANKS

Your sister is your other self.
She is your alter ego, your
reflection, your foil, your shadow.
She can represent both sides
of you at the same time, thus
throwing you into an emotional tailspin.
You are different in detail of
how you live your lives,
but not in substance.

BARBARA MATHIAS

A sister is the best there is. The absolute best.
And I appreciate everything about her:
her beautiful spirit, the intertwining of our lives,
and the way she brings so many smiles my way.

LAUREL ATHERTON

A sister is a friend
who has the ability to be impartial yet honest,
loyal yet independent, true yet fair,
and always compassionate.

LINDA BROWN

momentary sisters

*T'was her thinking of others
that made you think of her.*
ELIZABETH BROWNING

just a moment

Some sisters are only for a moment. Two women move, each along her own course of life, then ... a brief glance and shoulders brush. Somehow, in the flash of that moment, a kindred understanding transpires. It may be the comforting touch of an emergency room nurse as your frightened child is mended. Or the knowing smile of a classy, older woman in the checkout line as you discreetly attempt to discipline your unruly four-year-old. Perhaps it's a professional woman's concerned eyes that meet yours across a tense conference room. Somehow you know she understands.

She thinks like you do.

It can happen in all sorts of places and at various stages of life, yet somehow you know intuitively that this is a woman who understands what you're going through—a woman you can relate to.

39

How precious are these moments! Like priceless jewels, they encourage our hearts when we need it most. For it's in those difficult situations that we most need—and appreciate—small acts of kindness. Afterwards, we bless that sweet "sister" who took the time to show us kindness. We remember her for days, even years, to come.

Consider what little effort it takes to reach out to a sister in need: offer to hold a fussy baby while the flustered mother fumbles in her purse for her checkbook. Smile encouragement at a young woman who's obviously down on her luck. Gently squeeze an elderly woman's hand.

They may only be small tokens of love, yet they mean so much.

What a wonderful gift to share passing moments of sister-hood with other women along life's way. It's hard to tell who is most blessed—the one who receives, or the one who gives.

Kind words can be short
and easy to speak but their
echoes are truly endless.

MOTHER TERESA

immediate friends

I was far from home and feeling lonely when I learned by a late night-phone call that my dog (a dear sweet mutt of sixteen years) had just been put to sleep—and I hadn't even had the chance to pat his head or say good-bye.

Very early, the next morning, I stepped out to a gray, rainy day in Washington DC, my eyes still puffy from crying the night before. Mentally preparing myself to face a television camera interview, I tried to appear cheerful to the woman who arrived to escort me through my day.

42

When she asked how I was, I blurted out what had happened to my dog (instantly feeling foolish and longing to retract my overly emotional words). But she understood. Completely. She told me a few sad dog-stories herself and, immediately, I knew we were friends.

This dear little woman shuttled me all over Washington DC that day, getting me to interviews as well as local sights, and offering kind words of encouragement and sympathy all along the way. Then, as if she understood my needs better than I, she allowed me a couple of undisturbed hours in one of the most beautiful art museums I've been privileged to visit.

Like an angel of mercy, this woman ministered to my needs, then sent me on my way flying back home. I spent only a day with her, and will probably never meet her again. And yet, I feel a connection of momentary sisterhood I shall never forget.

Thank you for your generous kindness, Lottie!

43

When I have opened
my heart to a friend, I am
more myself than ever.
THOMAS MOORE

A helping word to one
in trouble is often like a
switch on a railroad track:
An inch between wreck and
smooth, rolling prosperity.

HENRY WARD BEECHER

A friend to Remember

She seemed very old to me, at the time, for I was only eighteen and anyone over thirty was ancient. But as I recall, she was in her sixties—and actually quite young for her age. We were to be "roomies" for six months. We'd both traveled from our homes in another country to lend a helping hand in a struggling third-world culture. We often joked that we were an odd pair—she was sure she was the oldest volunteer, and I was probably the youngest.

But this dear woman became a friend I will always remember. A southern lady, she was wise and witty, always ready to listen to my post-adolescent woes. She never lectured or preached but always had a kind word of encouragement laced with light humor. Although I only knew her for a few short months, I treasure her memory. I would be proud to be like her when I reach those golden years.

Kind words are
never wasted.
Like scattered seeds,
they spring up in
unexpected places.

E. M. BOUNDS

women Helping women

How I long to be the type of a woman who is willing to smile at a stranger, quick to offer an encouraging word, and ready to roll up her sleeves and pitch in. Yet how often I hesitate—second-guessing my motives, wondering if someone will think I'm presumptuous or if I'll offend the woman I'm trying to help.

I have to remind myself that even a bumbling kindness is better than kindness withheld. And besides, we can only improve with practice, right? So a few weeks ago, I offered to hold a crying baby in the doctor's waiting room while the nervous mother filled in her insurance forms. To my surprise, the baby even quieted down by the time his mother was ready to take him back. Our eyes met for a brief instant, and she realized someone cared about her—someone who had been a young mother once too.

47

Now that my children are grown and my days have taken on a less demanding pace, I'm asking God to make me more aware of the women I meet in the course of my life, perhaps for only a few minutes or hours. When a sister in need crosses my path I want to be sensitive to her feelings, and responsive to God's leading. I hope I will reach out in kindness and love, as so many others have reached out to me.

For the act of sisterhood has been passed down through the ages. Women have helped women throughout history. In fact, it's only in recent years that women have become less dependent on other women. We no longer rely on older women to help us through childbirth, or with the care of our little ones. When life begins to close in on us we feel like we must be strong and walk tall through our problems ... alone. But when we become too self-sufficient, we miss out on the joys and rewards of sisterhood. That's not just sad, it's tragic.

Come on girls. Let's reach out TO each other. Let's be there FOR each other.

Drop a stone into the water—
In a moment it is gone,
But there are a hundred ripples
Circling on and on and on—
Say a word of cheer and splendor—
In a moment it is gone,
But there are a hundred ripples
Circling on and on.
ANONYMOUS

Little kindnesses
. . .will broaden
your heart.
ZADIK

secret sisters

*Love is not premeditated—it is spontaneous,
it bursts forth in extraordinary ways.*
OSWALD CHAMBERS

secret surprises

*I*f you've ever planned a surprise party or a secret act of kindness, you know how much fun all the preparation and build-up of suspense can be. Then standing on the sidelines and watching the whole thing unfold is absolutely incredible! When you put kind thoughts, energy, and creativity into giving an anonymous gift or doing a secret act of kindness —*it's nothing short of thrilling!*

There are many ways to become a "secret sister." But how do you begin? First of all, ask God to lead you to someone who could use a blessing. Perhaps a neighbor, a co-worker, your child's teacher, or the harried clerk at the convenience store. Maybe you already know exactly who you'd like to bless.

51

Now, once you know *who* you want to bless, what do you do? How do you go about it? First of all, keep it a secret. That's all part of the fun and the challenge! Especially when you'll want to find out what she needs or would enjoy receiving without asking her directly. Quiz some of her friends or family. Gather information about her favorite colors, favorite authors or recording artists. Does she enjoy collecting certain items? Does she have a longing for a special something? You'll have to do some creative sleuthing.

Now the fun is in finding just the right item, wrapping it up beautifully, and arranging for an anonymous delivery. Remember that secret sister gifts don't have to be big and expensive. Even a small thoughtfulness is guaranteed to bring joy every time because it comes from the heart…with no strings attached!

A single violet, given
with love, is better than
a dozen perfect roses,
presented with indifference.
ANONYMOUS

52

surrounded by simple blessings

Have you ever paused to consider the big and little blessings that flow in and out of your life? Have you considered where they originated? Who's behind them? Obviously, we can give God credit for all our blessings—because "every good and perfect gift flows from the heavens above." But we also know that He often uses human hands and hearts. Sometimes He uses people close to home who bless our lives in personal ways, and sometimes He uses complete strangers.

Too often we don't think how people all around us are blessing our lives with little acts of kindness. Perhaps it's a thoughtful neighbor who turns off a hose that's left running, or a postman who hand-delivers an oversized package, or the lady in the Toyota who lets us merge into rush hour traffic in front of her.

53

Whether we notice or not, people all around us are doing little acts of courtesy and kindness—not to receive recognition but simply because they want to.

Have there been times when you wondered if someone was helping you in secret? Maybe it was that "serendipitous coincidence" when you thought you'd been incredibly fortunate, lucky, or blessed. But what if someone was behind the scenes all along, making it possible? We may never know for sure, but it gives us something to think about— and aspire to.

54

A perfect Rose

Dressed in worn and faded, ragged clothes,
In her wilted hand one ruby rose.
She bears her precious treasure with such care,
That people pause to glance, and some to stare.
Was it stolen from the city park—
Taken late at night when it was dark?
Surely, this old woman couldn't grow
Such a rose as this, you all must know.
The woman makes her way across the street,
To the corner where the *sad ones* meet.
She stops and looks into the stranger's eyes
Then with a smile, she gives the girl the prize.
The girl lights up as if she understands,
She cups the bright red
flower in both hands.
And God looks down and
smiles because He knows
This ragged woman is
His perfect Rose.

*No joy can equal the joy
of serving others.*

SAI BABA

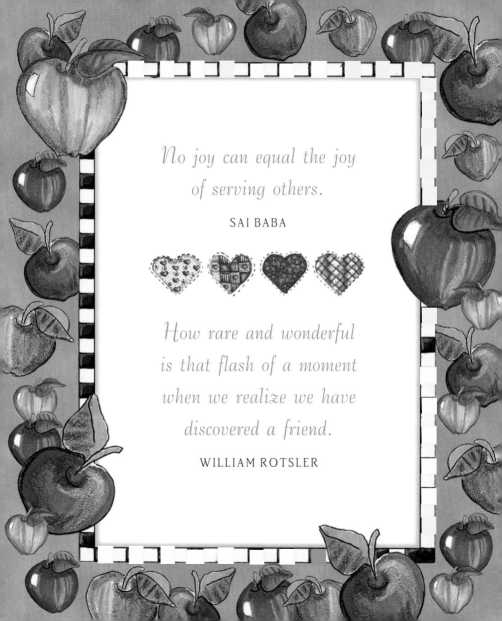

*How rare and wonderful
is that flash of a moment
when we realize we have
discovered a friend.*

WILLIAM ROTSLER

Random Kindness

While I appreciate the notion behind the book title, *Random Acts of Kindness*, I have to question it a bit. For I wonder: How is it possible for kindness to be done *randomly*? Isn't an act of kindness an intentional act that requires premeditation or at least a commitment to thoughtfulness? How can *that* be random?

Perhaps what the author intended to suggest was that kindness can be done here and there, throughout one's day in a random sort of way. And, I must agree, that's a wonderful idea—one that Jesus taught, in fact, when He spoke of being a good Samaritan or giving in secret or blessing your enemies.

The beauty comes when we make these kind acts *appear* to be random (like doing a good deed or letting someone else have the closer parking space). But I think it takes a little planning and preparation.

What if we all agreed to perform at least one act of kindness to a "secret sister" each day. Can you imagine how our world would change? How our perspective of life would improve?

How those around us would be blessed?

What if the next time we were in a hurry, driving somewhere and running late, we decided to take a deep breath, slow down a bit, and watch for ways to show kindness? Our heart rates might slow down, our blood pressures might drop, and we would probably find ourselves relaxing and smiling more. What fun that would be!

Thoughtful Acts
of Kindness

Ruthlessly clean your closet,
then donate used clothing to
a shelter for abused
women.

Invite your neighbor
over for coffee or tea.

Call your mother, or your aunt, or your
sister, or your niece— and just chat.

Offer to watch a harried
mom's kids, for free!

Bake something yummy
and share it anonymously
at work or with a neighbor.

Smile at the skateboard kids
hanging out on the corner.

Tell someone who waits on you
that they're doing a great job.

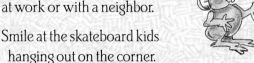

Visit an elderly shut in and listen to
her stories of "the good ol' days."

Write a thank-you note to someone
who's been influential in your life.

Start a Secret Sisters group
at work or in your church.

Leave an unusually big tip to the waitress who
looks like she's having a really bad day.

Compliment a co-worker
while the boss is listening.

Ask the cashier at the checkout stand
how she's doing today, then listen to her answer.

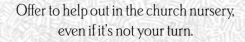

Offer to help out in the church nursery,
even if it's not your turn.

the sweet joy of giving

*I*t's really no secret, is it? The question of who is more blessed in the act of giving? Is it the one who receives or the one who gives? No doubt the one receiving thinks she is more blessed because she is grateful for the gift. Yet, even if the receiver is immensely blessed beyond wildest imagining, and even if she's wholeheartedly thankful for the gift—the giver is still *more* blessed!

Why? Ask yourself: What is equal to the pleasure of giving to someone in need? What brings greater delight than reaching out to another in love? Or sharing from your abundance? What reward is better than a thankful smile,

62

a grateful hand, or a softened heart? Can you think of anything more fulfilling?

When God has blessed us abundantly (both in material possessions and His love) how can we afford *not* to give our blessings away? He has been so generous with us, doesn't it make us want to help someone else? And when we do, He blesses us all over again!

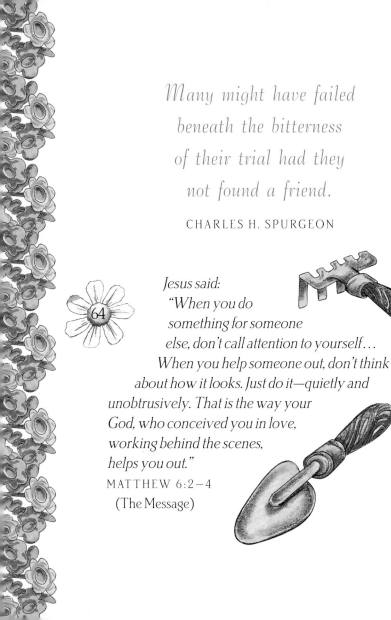

Many might have failed
beneath the bitterness
of their trial had they
not found a friend.

CHARLES H. SPURGEON

Jesus said:
"When you do
something for someone
else, don't call attention to yourself...
When you help someone out, don't think
about how it looks. Just do it—quietly and
unobtrusively. That is the way your
God, who conceived you in love,
working behind the scenes,
helps you out."
MATTHEW 6:2—4
(The Message)

younger sisters

*Friendship is . . .a
reward from the past, an
enrichment of the present,
and a legacy for the future.*
JUDITH J. YERMAN

Still a Little Girl

Beneath a veneer of dewy skin,
She's pensive, insecure, wondering;
She doubts herself; questions her ability
To fit into this "grown-up" world—
To *pass* for someone with answers,
knowledge, experience.
Yet on the outside, she wears her boldness
Like a cape of hot-pink confidence,
Flaunting it with youthful flare,
Parading her facade of self-assurance,
head held high—
but feeling like she's tripping along
in Mommy's high-heeled pumps
And desperately hoping no one will suspect,
No one will know
That beneath it all,
She's still a little girl.

Hands Held Across the Years

There's a certain irony about being a young woman—a paradox of sorts. As young women, we try to effuse an air of confidence. After all, we're just embarking on life. We have our dreams to pursue; our youthful good looks and health to buoy our spirits. Or as my wise grandmother used to warn: "You think you've got the world by the tail." But who wants to hold onto the tail if it happens to belong to a wild lion? And what happens if you let go? That's why underneath those smooth veneers of youthful radiance beat insecure hearts.

Being young can be overwhelming. Because, it's true, we *want* to know it all, we even *pretend* to know it all, but we know better than anyone else just how ill-prepared for life we are. Sometimes we long for an older "sister," a mature woman, to walk us gently through life's tough spots. But dare we admit our insecurities? Dare we humble

67

ourselves and ask for help? Goodness, no! For we're young—
time is on our side. We'll figure things out for ourselves. At least
we hope we will . . .

So how does an older sister stretch out her hand and
bridge the gap to the younger? How does she reach out,
across the generations, beyond the distance of years, time,
and experience? And how does the younger sister swallow
her youthful pride and ask for, even accept, help from the
one who has gone before?

Through love—the kind of love Jesus exhibited
when He crossed dimensions and generations to
dwell with mankind on earth. He set the pattern
when He humbled Himself and became like us
so we could trust and accept Him as a real and
lasting friend. In essence, He became our "older"
brother.

We women—younger sisters and older sisters—need
each other. We need to reach out to each other with empathy,
grace, and humor. To build a relationship founded on love. Let's
trust each other. Let's accept each other. And though it may
seem impossible at times, let's try to understand each other.
If nothing else, let's concentrate on what we have in common:
We're women! We're sisters at heart!

Younger Sister

Every time I look at you I see
Hope and expectation in your eyes,
Everything you think your life will be,
All the dreams you hope to realize.

Though I hope good things will come your way,
Time has taught me: not all dreams come true.
Still I must not fill you with dismay,
For I know the Lord can see you through.

And if you ever need a helping hand
Or someone you can tell your troubles to,
I promise that I'll try to understand,
Because I used to be a lot like you.

young at Heart

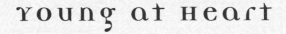

I recently read a list of ten things that supposedly "keep people youthful." Now, while I think youth has been highly overrated and I find absolutely nothing wrong with aging, I *do* want to remain *young at heart.* So I confess, I read the list.

One item that caught my attention was the suggestion that we remain youthful by "spending time with younger friends." I thought about that with great interest, for while in years past my friends have all been older than me, in recent years I've added some very dear friends who are quite a bit younger—which sometimes makes me feel pretty old! Like a few months ago when I was matron of honor for a friend of mine—a sweet, young woman seventeen years my junior! I felt sort of old and silly, but at the same time, I felt a bit younger, too. I felt connected to her generation and remembered how I'd been at that age: overwhelmed by the tumultuous emotions of the moment.

When we befriend a younger sister, we can't help but remember that we've been where she is. We've felt similar feelings; we've gone through similar difficulties. We can't help but identify and relate. Suddenly, we discover how much we have in common and find we have womanly wisdom to share! It dawns on us that we've actually learned a few things along life's highway—things learned only through experience and time.

It's not that we need to have all the answers, we simply need the courage and confidence to pat a younger sister on the arm, and say, "I know just how you feel, and I assure you it will get better." We older sisters have so much wisdom and warmth to share with our "younger sisters" who are just beginning their marriages, their families. What comfort and nurturing we can impart.

Who knows, maybe in the process these friendships will slow the aging process for us. But even if they don't prevent wrinkles or gray hair, at least they'll keep us young at heart!

To be able to find joy in another's joy,
that is the secret of happiness.
GEORGE BERNANOS

An Encouraging Word

Sometimes one small word of encouragement to a younger sister can make a world of difference. We may not even recall our actual words—but they can change a life forever. I know they changed mine.

I was just beginning to write, and time after time my work was sent back with a rejection letter. I felt dejected. I wanted to give up. I started to believe that publishing, for me, was an impossible, unattainable dream. But then God sent an older sister to encourage me—and *that* made all the difference!

Just when I thought I would never see my writing in print, I met an editor who encouraged me. Lonnie took the time to *read* my work and told me *she liked it!* She even promised to present it to her publishing committee. The fact that she took

73

the time to show an interest in my work meant so much to me.

When Lonnie showed me that she believed in me, everything changed. It was like a shot in the arm. I became more determined than ever, writing furiously and sending every new book proposal her way. Yet each time Lonnie took my proposals to her committee —they were rejected. Well, all except for one…

74

And now, more than sixty books later, I still jokingly tell Lonnie that she's the person who discovered me. She spoke words of encouragement when I was the most discouraged. And how thankful I am that she did!

Every time we encourage someone
we give them a transfusion of courage.
CHUCK SWINDOLL

To have friends,
One must first be friendly.
PROVERBS 18:24

A cheerful Heart

As a woman grows older she finds the differences between older women and younger women fewer and fewer. Why is that? Might there be a thing or two a younger sister knows that the older one has forgotten? Like how to laugh out loud and have fun without feeling guilty? Is there something the older sister can learn from the younger? Like being reminded of youthful optimism? Or the importance of cherished dreams, high hopes, and great expectations?

This reminds me of one of my favorite fiction characters—Anne Shirley of *Green Gables*—and the way she came into old spinster Marilla Cuthbert's life and totally rocked her world. Right from the start, Marilla was determined to change Anne into a good and sensible girl. But in the end, it was Marilla who was changed. Anne's sweet spirit and cheerful heart infected Marilla's life with laughter and love!

The writer of Proverbs says that a rejoicing heart and good news make our bones healthy. Although I've never completely understood this from a medical perspective, it does give me an idea…

Isn't it true that as women advance in age they often experience bone ailments like osteoporosis and arthritis? And wouldn't an older woman welcome some "health to her bones" if she's suffering from these afflictions?

How wonderful it would be to have our younger sisters bring "health to our bones." Perhaps younger women can take time to link arms with their "older" sisters and share a good belly laugh, a little merriment, some happiness and joy. After all, they'll be older women themselves one day. We're all part of the circle of sisterhood, quickly passing from younger sister to older, and the measure we give to others is the measure we'll receive. So let's all give cheerfully with hearts and arms open wide.

If there is any kindness
I can show, or any good thing
I can do to any fellow being,
let me do it now, and
not deter or neglect it,
as I shall not pass
this way again.

WILLIAM PENN

older sisters

*No love, no friendship,
can cross the path of our
destiny without leaving some
mark on it forever.*
FRANÇOIS MAURIAC

a tribute to sisterhood

uth speaks to Naomi—"Entreat me not to leave you, or to turn back from following after you; For wherever you go, I will go; and wherever you lodge, I will lodge; your people shall be my people, and your God, my God. Where you die, I will die, and there will I be buried." (Ruth 1:16—17 NKJV).

Don't we marvel at Ruth's devotion to her mother-in-law, Naomi? What an amazing friendship they shared! The story of Ruth's willingness to forsake her homeland and travel with Naomi is a timeless tribute to sisterhood. Yet I don't wonder at Ruth's loyalty, for the friendship of a loving older woman like Naomi— a woman so godly, so faithful, so kind —is a rare gift indeed. It's a privilege to spend time with such women for they encourage us to follow God with sincere hearts, to be all that we were meant to be, to love wholly and live fully.

I have a special reason to be thankful for these "older sisters." You see, I was raised in a single-parent home without a

functioning marriage relationship to observe, and my mother, who worked full-time, had little energy for domesticity. So I found myself sadly lacking when it came to the most basic homemaking skills. Yet I longed to be a good wife and mother, to run a household smoothly. I wanted to plant a garden, preserve jams, put up peaches, and make homemade soup that actually tasted good. But I had no idea where to begin.

That's when God sent a dear woman to be my friend. Only a few years older than me, *but oh so much wiser,* it seemed there was nothing she couldn't do. She was fun and creative too! But best of all, she had a heart set on serving God, which flowed onto everything she did. I can't count the times we shared the trials and triumphs of raising our families.

Now, even many years and miles later, I'm so grateful for my dear friend Kathy. I thank God for giving me this "older sister" just when I needed her most!

81

When I needed encouragement, you gave
me a pep talk
When I required help, you rolled up
your sleeves
When I wanted to talk, you picked up the phone
When I needed a hug, you opened your arms
When I had to vent, you lent me your ears
When I needed a nudge, you gave me an elbow
When I required correction, you did it ever
so gently
When I all I could do was cry,
you cried right along with me
And when I needed to pray,
you opened your heart

womanly wisdom

*I*n the book of Proverbs we're encouraged to seek wisdom as if we're looking for a lost treasure worth millions. But where do we go to seek wisdom? And how do we know when we find it?

Ironically, wisdom, though more rare than knowledge, can be found in the most common places. You might find it living right next door in the form of an elderly woman who has endured unspeakable hardships yet remains free of bitterness. Perhaps you will find it in the form of an aunt, a mother, or a grandmother. Maybe you've recognized wisdom in the eyes of the grocery store clerk, the woman who does your hair, or the eccentric artist with too many cats. Wisdom comes in all shapes and sizes, and, not unlike a buried treasure, is often found where you least expect it.

83

My grandmother was one of the wisest women I've known, though I'm certain she didn't think so, for she was always quick to admit her shortcomings and laugh at her own mistakes—which, of course, was part of her wisdom. When I think of my grandmother's wisdom, I think of the summers I spent in her care.

On many of those long, sultry afternoons, she combed her hair, put on a hat, and went *visiting*. She took me by the hand as we traipsed all over town to have tea with her friends. Elderly women like Belle Knife, a retired schoolteacher confined to a wheelchair. Or Clara, the white-haired lady who's house smelled like cabbage. Or Violet, who was short and round like her dachshund. They were all older than my grandmother (which made them quite ancient to me); they were wise, witty, full of interesting tales—and a bit lonely, I think. Grandmother would sip her tea and listen to them. She was never in a hurry and was genuinely interested in what they had to say. Which, now that I think of it, was probably why Grandmother was so wise.

What do we live for,
if it is not to make
life less difficult
for others.

GEORGE ELIOT

friendship from the heart

I remember the first time I met my husband's aunt Connie. It was my wedding day, and somehow I knew from the start this woman was special. I'd heard a little about her—how she had two grown sons, kept a beautiful home, was given to hospitality and kindness, loved to garden, and had built her own deck! I'd heard how all the kids in my husband's family loved and respected her.

Sadly, I only got to enjoy her company on rare occasions for she lived a hundred miles away, and I was soon busy raising two sons of my own, gardening, being hospitable, keeping house, and building decks... Two parallel lives, set apart in time and space—but similar somehow, kindred —as if I was following her example without even realizing it.

Now my two sons are grown. Connie has lots of delightful grandchildren—and cancer. For over a year now, her days have been "numbered"—though God alone knows the *real* number. Yet despite her pain, she remains a striking example of a godly woman. Her faith is stronger than ever, her enthusiasm contagious, her love of life evident—only her body has slowed down a little, but not much.

Recently I took the opportunity to tell her just how much she has meant to me, to describe the quiet and profound impact she has had on my life. Of course, she just laughed, her eyes sparkling, incredulous that it could be true when we'd spent so little time together. But some things happen in a moment—in a flash. Some things you can't understand with your mind, you know them in your heart.

The language of friendship is not words, but meanings.
HENRY DAVID THOREAU

growing old graciously

I'm not sure if I'll wear purple when I'm old, but I might! And I might wear a straw hat covered with colorful flowers and go barefoot in the garden and strike up conversations with perfect strangers. I just might.

Though I'm still getting used to the idea of growing old (especially since it's inevitable), one thing is clear to me: I want to be an "older sister"—a mentor who reaches out to younger women and shares from the richness and wisdom of life. I've received so many blessings as a "younger sister." Now it's time for me to be an "older sister," to become more giving and more gracious.

89

That's how I think of "older sisters," for the women who touched my life the most—in thoughtful ways that changed me, challenged me, and made me a better person—were always *gracious.* They didn't lecture or preach or judge. They were nurturing, encouraging, and faithful. They simply opened their arms and accepted me in love.

That's how I want to grow old—*graciously.* With arms stretched out in love... even if I do wear crazy hats ... and purple.

The most precious
gift that one person
can bestow upon
another is gentle
encouragement.

PHILLIP KELLER

forever sisters

To get the full value of joy,
you must have someone to divide it with.
MARK TWAIN

friendship Grows sweeter

The really *best* of friends—the women who are closer than sisters—are those friends who've been through a lot together. They've enjoyed the good times, and comforted each other during the tough times. They're the ones you telephone to share some wonderful news; they're the ones you run to when your heart is breaking. You know they'll stick by you through thick or thin. They'll always be there.

They're also the ones you share the ordinary, everyday things of life with. You know they won't yawn with boredom when you tell them about Katie's first tooth or that Jamie is struggling in English or that your perennials just aren't blooming well this year.

This kind of friend will laugh at your jokes—or tell you they're not funny without hurting your feelings. She's the one you confide in when you're worried about your marriage, your finances, your health, your faith. You can be completely candid and honest, for you

93

know she won't judge you. When she gives you advice, you know it's worth listening to, for she has your best interests in mind.

Yet even the very best friend isn't perfect. Every friendship has its share of ups and downs, disappointments and discouragements. But the true test of friendship is whether it endures the hard times as well as the happy times.

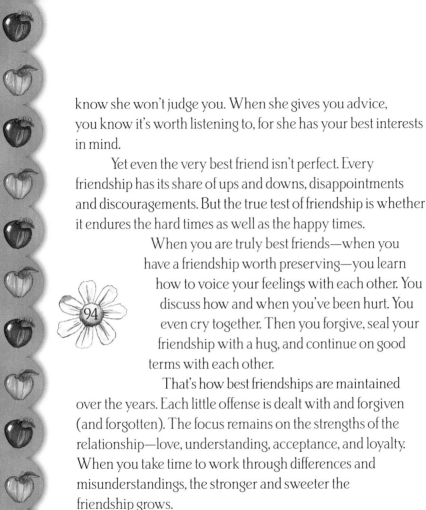

When you are truly best friends—when you have a friendship worth preserving—you learn how to voice your feelings with each other. You discuss how and when you've been hurt. You even cry together. Then you forgive, seal your friendship with a hug, and continue on good terms with each other.

That's how best friendships are maintained over the years. Each little offense is dealt with and forgiven (and forgotten). The focus remains on the strengths of the relationship—love, understanding, acceptance, and loyalty. When you take time to work through differences and misunderstandings, the stronger and sweeter the friendship grows.

Dear Friend,

We've been through so much together
The laughter, the blahs, and the tears,
My life would be boring without you,
What would I have done all those years?
I don't want to take you for granted,
Or ever forget to forgive,
For I hope that our friendship will last
Just as long as we both get to live.
And one day when I go to heaven,
(Hopefully when I'm very old,)
I'll say: "Thank you, Lord, for my sister,
She's been worth her weight in pure gold!"

A friend is one who makes me do my best.
OSWALD CHAMBERS

тhe gift of нer нeart

What if we had to pay our best friend by the hour for her counseling services? Do you think we'd all go broke? Maybe it would balance out—we'd trade services equally. What would life be like without a friend to listen to our complaints and concerns and longings?

Actually, a good friend is even better than a counselor because she doesn't have to sit down and take your case history; she already knows almost all there is to know—your weaknesses, your dreams, your struggles. And she understands and loves you just the same. You can trust her to give her best advice because she wants what's best for you.

And that's exactly the way you feel about her too. You want to be an empathetic listener, full of understanding and wisdom. Though you don't have all the answers, you offer hope and encouragement and support. Then you promise to pray.

A truly good friend cares about you so much she's willing to lay your friendship on the line. She's willing to tell you the truth, even when it hurts—or isn't what you want to hear. She'll wrap the truth in a thick layer of love, but she won't hesitate to be honest and candid when she knows that's what you need to hear.

A true friend will speak up if she feels you're dating the wrong guy or being too hard on your husband or letting a job stress you out. She sees your blind-spots—those areas of life you prefer to overlook or deny. A true friend will speak out, even if she risks offending you because she cares about you. And she knows that in time you'll come to your senses, forgive her, and even thank her!

Whether you're hearing the hard truth or giving it, be willing to take a risk. That's how you become a true friend. And any friendship worth keeping is worth risking.

A mere friend will agree with you,
but a real friend will argue.
RUSSIAN PROVERB

A friend is one to whom we may pour out all the contents of our hearts, chaff and grain together knowing that the gentlest of hands will take and sift it, keep what is worth keeping and with a breath of kindness blow the rest away.

ARABIAN PROVERB

A sister of the Heart

A best friend—a sister of the heart—is a priceless treasure. And like a rare jewel, her value appreciates over time. In other words, she's worth hanging on to! Friendships like that don't come along every day, and that's why they're worth all the time and energy you can invest in them. In fact, the more you invest in them the more valuable they become.

But what happens when hundreds or even thousands of miles separate you from a friend you hold dear? You'll need to take special measures to keep the doors of communication open. Like a priceless jewel, you'll need to give the friendship a little buffing and polishing from time to time, so it doesn't lose it's splendor and grow dull.

How do you maintain a long-distance friendship? Through letters, telephone calls, e-mails, cards, gifts, and a visit from time to time. You can also pray for each other no matter how many miles separate you.

However you choose to do it, keep in touch! For just as a rare jewel is most precious to the owner who understands its value, so is a treasured friend. Don't let the distance between you be anything other than miles!

100

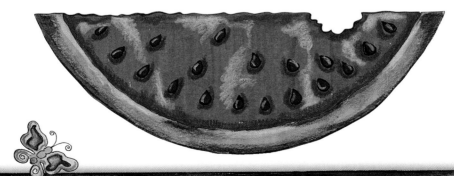

There is no friend like an old friend
Who has shared our morning days.
No greeting like [her] welcome,
No homage like [her] praise.

OLIVER WENDELL HOLMES

Love and Lasting Friendships

So what is the key to friendship? What one quality or characteristic do you look for? Do you seek out loyalty? forgiveness? compassion? humility? integrity? faithfulness? availability? humor? empathy? cheerfulness? If you could pick only one trait to have in a friend, which one would you choose? While all these qualities are wonderful and valuable to any relationship, there is still another characteristic that is necessary to sustain a friendship through anything and everything—and that's *love*.

Love has so many qualities all wrapped up in one amazing package; it's almost impossible to define. But if anything can make a friendship lasting and worthwhile, it's love. In fact, a friendship without love is really a mere acquaintance. Even the most casual friendships are made up of at least a small amount of love. And the friendships we cherish the most always begin and end in love.

102

A Foolproof Formula
for Friendship

Love never gives up.
Love cares more for others than for self.
Love doesn't want what it doesn't have.
Love doesn't strut,
Doesn't have a swelled head,
Doesn't force itself on others,
Isn't always "me first,"
Doesn't fly off the handle,
Doesn't keep score of the sins of others,
Doesn't revel when others grovel,
Takes pleasure in the
flowering of truth,
Puts up with anything,
Trusts God always,
Always looks
for the best,
Never looks back,
But keeps going
to the end.

I CORINTHIANS 13
(The Message)

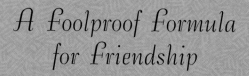

Dear God,
Teach me to value my friend in the way that you value me:
You gave your all for me.
Help me to forgive my friend in the way that you forgive me:
Completely.
Show me how to serve my friend in the way that you serve me:
Humbly.
Fill me with love for my friend in the way that you love me:
Unconditionally.
Remind me that whatever I do for my friend, I also do for you.
Amen.

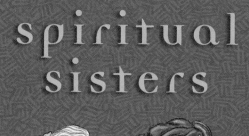

spiritual
sisters

A friend loves at all times . . .

PROVERBS 17:17

blood sisters

Did you ever have a best friend in childhood—someone so special you wished she was your real sister, and you wondered if perhaps your parents might adopt her, or hers would take you in? Perhaps to seal your friendship, like Tom and Huck, you stabbed your forefingers with a pin and pressed them together to become honest-to-goodness "blood sisters."

When you think back on that childhood ritual it seems a bit barbaric. After all, a good friendship isn't established by the shedding of blood. Or is it?

There is *someone* (someone closer than a brother) who has spilled His blood so that we might be adopted into His family. *Someone* who willingly laid down His life for us—so that we might experience true love and forgiveness.

When Jesus bled and died on the cross, He united us to His Father, to Himself, and to each other. Only through His sacrifice can we become true spiritual sisters. In essence, Jesus is the one who miraculously makes us "blood sisters." We don't need to prick our fingers, we simply need to allow His blood to cleanse us and to unite us with Him and each other. Then we are truly *blood sisters.*

Greater love has no one than this, that he lay down his life for his friends.
JOHN 15:13

The more we love, the better we are;
and the greater our friendships are,
the dearer we are to God.
JEREMY TAYLOR

Held Together by Love

O nly a master stonemason can create a wall of various shapes and sizes of rocks without using mortar to hold them together. Yet a wall like this is one of the strongest known to mankind and can last for centuries.

As the mason carefully selects the odd-shaped stones, placing them together just so—a round stone fitting into a concave stone…a sharply indented stone fitting into the opposite indentations of another—the wall is strengthened by the irregularities. Occasionally the mason might use one stone to knock a jagged edge from another. Then he presses and grinds the stones into each other until they fit just right.

The Bible describes our lives as "living stones." God's skillful hands build us into a "living wall," interconnected with each other. He thoughtfully chooses us, one at a time, and then carefully fits us together—often placing someone with opposite characteristics next to us, so we will fit more tightly, more perfectly. It can be uncomfortable at times, when we are pressed and pushed together or when a sharp edge is ground down and softened by a "sister stone." But in the end, it's always worth it. For our "living wall" will endure—it will last throughout eternity.

You also, as living stones, are being built up a spiritual house, a holy priesthood, to offer up spiritual sacrifices acceptable to God through Jesus Christ.

1 PETER 2:4-5 NKJV

A friend is the hope of the heart.
RALPH WALDO EMERSON

sisters in god's family

Most of us have not been orphaned—left alone in the world to get by without help from our family. We've never felt that deep hunger and need for someone to adopt us, love us, make us their own. But, it's something we can relate to in the spiritual realm, for we've all felt that deep, heart-longing to know God as our Father, to become His precious child.

When we accept God's unconditional love, and receive His grace and forgiveness, we are miraculously adopted into His family. God, the King of all creation, reaches out His Father's hand to us, and we become *His children*—heirs to His eternal kingdom.

As if that's not enough, we also become members of a brand, new family, filled with lots of spiritual siblings, who like us, have been adopted as God's children. That's where true spiritual sisterhood begins—when we love and accept one another in the same way our Heavenly Father has loved and accepted us. Unconditionally and forever!

As spiritual sisters, we have an amazing connection that goes deeper than blood, lasts longer than physical life and is stronger

than the greatest friendship on earth. We are bound to each other by our Heavenly Father. Our spiritual sisterhood will last throughout all eternity!

I celebrate this spiritual connection with you, dear sister. I rejoice that we are part of God's family. I thank God that He is touching and changing us daily—molding and making us into His image. I see His resemblance in you.

Let's recommit our hearts to encourage one another to serve God faithfully in all that we do. Let's remind each other to keep our eyes steadfastly on Him, to listen eagerly to His voice, and to do His will gladly. Together, let's enjoy the blessings and grace that come with being daughters of the King. What an incredible inheritance we share, sister of mine!

A Prayer for My Sister

Dear God:
Pour out Your love on my sister,
And convince her of Your mercy.
Show her the path You would have her take,
And hold her hand along the way.
Comfort her in the dark of night,
And bring forth Your light in the morning.
Amen

Sisters at Heart ♥ Notes

Names & Addresses
of my Sisters at Heart ♥

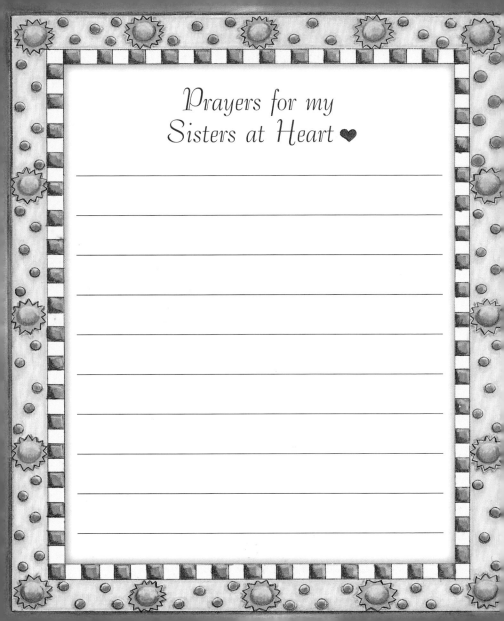

Prayers for my
Sisters at Heart ♥